FEATHERS AND TEETH

BY
CHARISE CASTRO SMITH

★

★

DRAMATISTS
PLAY SERVICE
INC.

NOTE ON BILLING

Anyone receiving permission to produce FEATHERS AND TEETH is required to give credit to the Author as sole and exclusive Author of the Play on the title page of all programs distributed in connection with performances of the Play and in all instances in which the title of the Play appears, including printed or digital materials for advertising, publicizing or otherwise exploiting the Play and/or a production thereof. Please see your production license for font size and typeface requirements.

Be advised that there may be additional credits required in all programs and promotional material. Such language will be listed under the "Additional Billing" section of production licenses. It is the licensee's responsibility to ensure any and all required billing is included in the requisite places, per the terms of the license.

SPECIAL NOTE ON SONGS/RECORDINGS

Dramatists Play Service neither holds the rights to nor grants permission to use any songs or recordings mentioned in the Play. Permission for performances of copyrighted songs, arrangements or recordings mentioned in this Play is not included in our license agreement. The permission of the copyright owner(s) must be obtained for any such use. For any songs and/or recordings mentioned in the Play, other songs, arrangements, or recordings may be substituted provided permission from the copyright owner(s) of such songs, arrangements or recordings is obtained; or songs, arrangements or recordings in the public domain may be substituted.

FEATHERS AND TEETH was produced in a developmental production in Goodman Theatre's 2014 New Stages Festival and received its world premiere at Goodman Theatre (Robert Falls, Artistic Director; Roche Schulfer, Executive Director), Chicago, Illinois on September 19, 2015. It was directed by Henry Godinez; the set design was by Kevin Depinet; the sound design was by Mikhail Fiksel; the lighting design was by Jesse Klug; the costume design was by Christine Pascual; the casting was by Adam Belcuore and Erica Sartini-Combs; the Foley artist was Carolyn Ann Hoerdemann; the dramaturg was Tanya Palmer; and the production stage manager was Kimberly Osgood. The cast was as follows:

CAROL .... Christina Hall
ARTHUR .... Eric Slater
CHRIS .... Olivia Cygan
HUGO SCHMIDT .... Jordan Brodess
ELLIE .... Ali Burch

CHARACTERS

CAROL, 32. Coiffed like Farrah Fawcett.

ARTHUR, 40. A higher-up at one of the factories in town. Not the highest-up.

CHRIS, 13. Sullen.

HUGO SCHMIDT, 11. German.

TIME AND PLACE

The play takes place in the spring of 1978, in a factory town in the Midwest. The stage is split between the very modern kitchen of an upper-middle-class home, and the crawl space under the house, directly below the kitchen. In the kitchen, there are wallpapered walls, linoleum floors, and a lot of wood paneling. There's a steel sink below a window with curtains. A table with three chairs is center stage. Stage right is the entrance to the house. Stage left is the door to the backyard. The crawl space below is just leftover insulation, some tarps and dirt.

NOTE

This play is to be played a little broadly. The characters are just slightly larger than life. All of them (with the exception of Chris) probably wish that they were characters on *The Brady Bunch*. There might even be laugh tracks. They all proceed with the mindset that everything will turn out right in the end, until that becomes impossible.

FEATHERS AND TEETH

Scene 1

Carol's real done up, for someone who's sitting in a kitchen on a weekday evening. She's got a pot roast in the oven. She smokes a cigarette and reads National Geographic. *The front door of the house opens offstage. She perks up.*

CAROL. Chris?

No response.

Chris hon, is that you?

Silence.

Hon?

Carol walks offstage and finds the front door open.

Chris? You gotta remember to close the door when you come in, okay hon?
Chris? Hon?

CHRIS. OKAY!!

Silence.

CAROL. You got any schoolwork tonight?
I can help you with your schoolwork if you want.

No response. The oven starts to smoke, she doesn't notice.

Okay, well you just let me know if you want help.
I'm making a pot roast.
I just hope you haven't spoilt your appetite on hamburgers!

Silence. A door slams upstairs. Loud music starts to play from a record player upstairs—a classic rock song like Led Zeppelin's

*"When the Levee Breaks."**

Carol smells the smoke, runs over to the oven and opens it. The pot roast is burnt, black. Unsalvageable. Smoke pours out of the oven into the kitchen. The smoke detector starts to go off.

Oh, for crying out loud!

She reaches into the oven impulsively with no mitts on. She burns her hands, lets out a tiny cry, then shoves her hands between her legs, determined not to scream. Very quietly—

Jesus Mary and Saint Joseph the carpenter!!

After the first wave of pain subsides, she removes her hands, looks at her fingers and blows on them gently.

She calmly gets potholders, removes the singed pot roast, and carries it out the back door of the house and hoists it out onto the lawn. She returns with the empty pot and places it in the sink.

She waves a tea towel in front of the smoke detector until the smoke dissipates and it shuts off.

The phone starts to ring. Carol answers it.

Hello?
Good afternoon Mrs. Schmidt.
No, everyone is all right.
False alarm.
Just ruined a pot roast I'm afraid! Hahaha!
Sorry to have alarmed you.
All right.
You take care now.
Goodbye.

She hangs up the phone, goes into the pantry, and retrieves a box of Hamburger Helper. Calls upstairs.

Change of plans sweetheart. I'm going to fix up some Hamburger Helper.

Silence.

Chris?
Is that all right?

* See special note on songs and recordings on copyright page.

6

No response. Carol goes to the fridge and takes out a package of ground beef to start in on the Hamburger Helper.

Carol unwraps the raw ground beef. She dumps it into a metal bowl to start prepping.

Then she very furtively wads some of it into a little ball and eats it.

Suddenly, the back door opens and slams shut. The music from upstairs stops. A man with a moustache, in a brown polyester three-piece suit, hurries in. His hands and forearms are dripping in blood.

Arthur!!!

What have you done ohmylord ARTHUR!!

ARTHUR. Now don't go getting excited Carol it's just a—

Arthur starts to look around the kitchen for something. Blood is getting everywhere.

CAROL. It's all over the kitchen now, Arthur! What have you done?

ARTHUR. I SAID IT'S NOTHING, CAROL.

I was pulling into the driveway and I hit—well, something got *stuck* under one of the tires and I tried to save it but—where's a bucket Carol?

CAROL. I just don't know what to make out of this Arthur. There's blood all over the floor.

ARTHUR. A bucket, Carol—

CAROL. I… I just did the floors this afternoon Arthur.

Carol is paralyzed, staring at the trail of blood on the floor. Arthur sighs and grabs the scorched pot out of the sink. He goes out the back door.

Where are you going with the—not the pot Arthur!

NOT THE POT!

Arthur returns carrying something in the pot. It's heavy for something small enough to be carried in a pot. Arthur heaves it onto the kitchen table.

WHAT ARE YOU DOING ARTHUR?!!?

I SAID NOT THE POT.

ARTHUR. It's still breathing. I couldn't just leave it there.

Silence. There is a small, injured whine from inside the pot.

CAROL. Well now. What is it then?

7

ARTHUR. It's dinged up pretty bad but ah, it's a possum Carol. We used to get possums out here all the time. Maybe a little possum. Or a squirrel most likely. I'm guessing it's either a possum, a squirrel, a little ferret, a fox, or a rat.

Carol looks into the pot. She recoils in horror.

CAROL. Oh NO Arthur.

ARTHUR. Like I said it's pretty dinged up.

CAROL. Oh Heavens Arthur.

ARTHUR. Nothing to be afraid of Carol. It's just a possum, a squirrel, a little ferret, a fox, a rat or a… Hold on a second Carol, are those feathers?

CAROL. A turkey maybe?

ARTHUR. Turkeys don't have—Oh for Pete's sake Carol—Turkeys don't have teeth. Like that.

There is another whine from inside the pot, more urgent. And a desperate scratching sound.

CAROL. Arthur, I think it's—is it scratching?

More scratching. It's trying to climb up the walls of the pot.

ARTHUR. Get me the lid, Carol.

CAROL. What?!?

ARTHUR. Don't make any sudden moves Carol. Just get me the lid.

Carol gets it together and hands Arthur the lid. The thing in the pot is still scratching and struggling to get out. Arthur creeps over to the pot and slams the lid down. There is an enraged snarl from inside the pot. It's struggling. Arthur has to really fight to keep the lid on.

CAROL. Oh my oh my oh my GOD Arthur!!

The thing in the pot makes one last attempt and then stops struggling.

Do you think it's passed Arthur?

ARTHUR. Your guess is as good as mine Carol.

There is a tiny whine from inside the pot.

CAROL. Oh. Well I guess it's still… amongst us.

ARTHUR. Maybe we should take it to the veterinarian?

CAROL. Maybe we should just put it to rest. Because it seems like it's in pain.

ARTHUR. Not to worry Carol, I'll just run it right over to the veterinarian.

> *Carol stares off, stoic.*

What?

CAROL. I think it might be an endangered species.

ARTHUR. Oh sweetheart, it's no danger to us.

Not in the shape that it's in, and not inside the pot.

CAROL. Well Arthur, it's just that... An endangered species is—I read about this in the *National Geographic*—an endangered species is when there's practically no animals left of a species. And I don't know exactly what this thing is, but I know I've never seen anything like it, so don't you think that maybe it might be endangered Arthur?

ARTHUR. Well then that's all the more reason for us to take it to the veterinarian Carol.

CAROL. Well here's just one small problem with that Arthur: According to the *National Geographic*, that son of a gun Nixon passed a law where if you harm an endangered species it's... well, you gotta go to jail.

ARTHUR. That son of a gun! They send you to jail Carol?

CAROL. Well, yes. I'm afraid that's the case. So.

> *The thing in the pot whines again. It's really pitiful, painful to listen to.*

ARTHUR. It just shot out of nowhere before I could hit the brakes.

CAROL. Oh no. This is terrible.

ARTHUR. I'm so sorry Carol.

> *Carol starts to cry in a really pretty way. Arthur goes to comfort her.*

CAROL. Arthur maybe could you—your hands still have the—

ARTHUR. Oh, right.

> *Arthur goes to the sink and starts to wash the blood off his hands.*

That's strange.

CAROL. What is?

ARTHUR. It's not coming off.

CAROL. Use the Palmolive.

ARTHUR. I did. But it's...

> *He sniffs his fingers.*

Sticky.

Carol sighs, "Oh, men," goes under the sink and takes out rubber gloves, some Ajax, and a scrub brush.

CAROL. Hold still.

Carol goes to town scrubbing Arthur's hands and arms.

ARTHUR. You see!

CAROL. Yeah I see what you mean. It *is* sticky.

The thing in the pot lets out the most desperate sound yet. Arthur and Carol turn around to face it, Arthur's arms still covered in blood, Carol's gloves now covered in blood as well. At this moment we should realize that Chris, dressed in a 1960s flower child muumuu, has been quietly watching them for some time.

CHRIS. So what's in the pot?

CAROL. Oh! Chris hon, it's just—your father accidentally hit an animal with his car.

ARTHUR. It's badly hurt, honey. It's not going to make it. But it's still alive. And so we're—

Chris goes to one of the kitchen drawers and pulls out a large carving knife. She's at the table in a flash, lifts the lid from the pot and stabs the thing in the pot over and over and over again. Arthur and Carol scream. The thing in the pot screams. Chris is calm.

Finally the thing in the pot stops screaming. Arthur and Carol stop screaming. They stare at Chris, who has blood splattered all over her face and arms. Chris drops the knife into the pot.

CHRIS. It's over now.

Arthur and Carol stare at her, slack-jawed.

Can we get some Chinese for dinner?

CAROL. Oh, Chris. Hon—

CHRIS. I've asked you to stop calling me hon, Carol. You're not my mom.

Chris turns and goes back upstairs.

Blackout.

Scene 2

A little while later, Carol, Arthur, and Chris sit around the dinner table with takeout containers of Chinese food. They've all still got spatters of blood on them because they couldn't scrub it off. Carol picks at her food. Arthur eats slowly. Chris eats with gusto, clacking her chopsticks.

CHRIS. Sure beats pot roast, right Dad?
ARTHUR. Christine, that's rude. Apologize to Carol.
CHRIS. Sorry Carol.
But I guess no more pot means no more pot roast—In the future.
Right Dad?

> *Arthur glares at her.*

…sorry Carol…
CAROL. Oh that's all right Chris.
It's only that… well I might as well tell you that was my mother…
my mother's pot.
CHRIS. Well this was my mother's house.
CAROL. It's solid cast iron Chris.
It gets seasoned over time. The more you use it, the better it gets.
My mother got that pot as a bride, cooked in it for forty years,
Then passed it down to me.
ARTHUR. Oh no, sweetheart. I had no idea.
CHRIS. Stop calling Carol sweetheart. It's disrespectful to Mom.
ARTHUR. Eat your food.
CAROL. It's all right Arthur. It's only a pot.

> *They eat in silence for a moment. Then Carol bursts into tears.*

Oh I guess there's no use in trying to hide it Arthur.
I am. I am heartsick over the pot.
We didn't have much back when I was growing up.
But my parents were hardworking and decent people.
And even when times were tough,
You could count on my mother to have a warm meal waiting in that pot.

11

I suppose that's why I'm so busted up over that pot Arthur.
I'd hoped that pot would be a source of comfort for our family too.
CHRIS. You aren't in our family.
ARTHUR. Yes she is Chris. We've been over this.
You know that Carol's a part of our family now.
CAROL. It's all right Arthur. She'll come around in time.
CHRIS. I'm sitting right here Carol. / I can hear you.
CAROL. And I suppose that really when you look at it,
Things will turn out right over the pot.
Because look at this beautiful house,
Look at the wonderful... bounty of things in this house.
You've been blessed to never know want the way I have Chris.
So maybe I'm just making a whole big racket over a silly old pot.

> *Carol laughs sweetly. Like it's all just been a big silly misunderstanding but, hey, lesson learned.*

ARTHUR. Carol you are a treasure.
You are just an absolute treasure.
CHRIS. I'm a treasure too though right Dad?
I also am a treasure.
CAROL. Of course you are a treasure Chris.
No one is saying that you're not.
CHRIS. Dad?
ARTHUR. Why don't you finish your supper Christine?
Before it gets cold.

> *Chris starts to make small anxious sounds under her breath. Like she's trying to self-soothe or something, but it's not working. Her sounds start to sound like the sounds the animal was making in the pot.*

CAROL. Chris, would you um—do you think you might stop that hon?
CHRIS. What?
CAROL. Those noises Christine, they're disturbing. And maybe your dad will back me up here—
I'm not so sure they're appropriate for the dinner table.
ARTHUR. She's right, knock it off Chris.
CHRIS. Dad, are we in China right now?
ARTHUR. What?
CHRIS. Are we in the United Soviet States of Russia?
CAROL. Of course not Christine. We're in America.

CHRIS. Okay. Well, just checking to make sure that we do actually live in a free country with free speech instead of an oppressive Communist regime where you're not allowed to make sounds that you feel like making at the dinner table.

Carol gets up and goes into the pantry.

ARTHUR. Carol, what are you doing?

CAROL. I need a flashlight Arthur.

ARTHUR. What for?

CAROL. And a shovel.

ARTHUR. There's one in the garage.

Carol starts to go.

What are you doing Carol?

CAROL. I want to give it a proper burial.

ARTHUR. Oh, honey. It's late already. It's dark out.

CAROL. That's why I need the flashlight.

ARTHUR. Why don't you wait until morning?

CAROL. I'd just like to put it to rest. So that other animals won't get at it.

CHRIS. Get at its dead body you mean?

Those other animals can dig, you know.

They can just dig it right up and eat it.

CAROL. That's why I'm going to make the hole very deep.

ARTHUR. I'll help you.

CAROL. That's okay Arthur. You finish your supper.

Carol finds a flashlight, heads out the back door. Chris stares at her father. Arthur avoids eye contact.

ARTHUR. Christine.

Where'd that dress come from?

CHRIS. My closet.

ARTHUR. Well how about you just put it in the wash and I'll run it down to the Salvation Army after work tomorrow.

CHRIS. Well how about let's not Dad.

ARTHUR. Don't start up again over this Christine.

We both know it's not healthy for you to be wearing Ellie's clothes around like this.

CHRIS. How about you just run Ellie's pictures and records and ashes down to the Salvation Army too while you're at it? That'd probably be real healthy too, right Dad?

13

ARTHUR. JESUS CHRISTINE!
I'm doing my best.
Cut me some goddam slack here!

>*Chris takes him in and cuts it out.*

CHRIS. I just don't want us to forget about Ellie, Dad.
ARTHUR. I haven't.
Christine, I want to say something to you—Carol and I have both
noticed this—
It seems like
Your behavior has been getting more and more... bizarre lately.
CHRIS. Bizarre?
ARTHUR. Like with that creature in the pot.
CHRIS. Well, it's just that I heard you and Carol talking about
how you'd better put it down and I didn't want to have to listen to
that sound it was making anymore so I just went for it. *Because that
thing in the pot made me sort of think about Mom, those last three
days.* And how she would have been better off dead than alive those
last three days. Just the same as the thing in the pot.
ARTHUR. ...
CHRIS. I just felt so sorry for it Dad. And so sad for it.

>*Chris starts to cry for real.*

ARTHUR. There, there now Christine. Don't you cry now.

>*Chris goes and sits on her father's lap and wraps her arms
>around his neck. He pats her back, although clearly this makes
>him uncomfortable.*

CHRIS. More of Ellie is missing every day.
You know that pearl necklace that she always used to wear?
ARTHUR. Sure do, Chris.
CHRIS. Well, it's gone.
It was on my dresser and now I can't find it.
And those pearls were really special because she loved them, and in
this whole entire world there will never be another necklace like that.
She gave it to me. And I lost it. And now that necklace is just as
gone as Ellie is.
ARTHUR. That necklace is going to turn up somewhere Christine.
That's a promise.
CHRIS. Sometimes I feel so sad about Mom,
It's like I've got a rock choking the life out of my heart.

ARTHUR. It's a… it's a hell of a thing to try to understand Christine.
We all… everybody loved Ellie, that's for sure.
But ah, you just have to try to ah, keep—
Keep looking on the bright side. Keep on… keeping on.

Arthur has completely talked himself into a corner.

CHRIS. I know you've been really busy with Carol these past two
months but,
I've really missed you Arthur.

*Chris softly, awkwardly attempts to kiss her father on the
cheek? The mouth? We can't tell and neither can he. Arthur is
shocked and pushes her off of him. Chris falls on the floor and
howls with rage.*

*Carol enters from the backyard, her hands and knees covered
in soil.*

CAROL. Arthur, what happened?
ARTHUR. Christine, I just—
What on earth were you thinking? I have *had* it!
Go to your room.

*Chris gets up, chucks a takeout container of Chinese food at
Carol, and runs offstage.*

Goddamit Carol! This is just a…
A Grade-A example of what I've been saying about Chris and her
acting out.
I don't know how much more of this I can put up with Carol.

Re: the General Tso's all over Carol's shirt:

Oh for Christ's sake Carol, let me get you a dishtowel or something.
CAROL. I'm fine Arthur, nothing a can of seltzer won't fix.
ARTHUR. She's out of control Carol!
I don't know what I'm supposed to do here.
CAROL. I'm sure she's just being a teenager Arthur. It's hormones.
It will pass.
ARTHUR. You think?

Carol shrugs.

So. You buried it?
CAROL. I did. At the base of the oak tree, right next to the grill.
ARTHUR. You buried it next to the grill?
CAROL. It was the only spot where there wasn't roots or lawn.

ARTHUR. What about your mother's wedding pot?
CAROL. I buried that too. I buried the poor thing inside the pot,
may it rest in peace.
ARTHUR. I really am sorry about the pot Carol.
CAROL. How could you have known Arthur?
ARTHUR. Still.

>*Pause.*

I've been thinking Carol,
That Chris's acting out episodes probably are on account of Ellie.
CAROL. Might *could* be…
ARTHUR. Well, just what am I supposed to do about that Carol?
It's not like I can bring Ellie back from the dead.
CAROL. Sure can't.
ARTHUR. Plenty of young girls' mothers die and probably most
of them don't go around stabbing poor innocent creatures in pots.
CAROL. I'm sure most don't, Arthur.
But just—try not to get too worked up about it. Okay?

>*She starts to rub his shoulders. He relaxes for just a moment.
>Then a song like Night Sun's "Living with the Dying" starts to
>blast from the record player upstairs.* *

ARTHUR. I tell you what Carol, I don't think those records are
helping any with Chris and her acting out.
CAROL. The rock and roll?
ARTHUR. I can't stand the sound of it. But Ellie loved all sorts of
music—that's how come she let Chris have those records. All of
this acting out might be that music she listens to.

>*Arthur stares off into space.*

CAROL. It might be, with Chris, I'm thinking that maybe part of
the acting out problem might be… me.
ARTHUR. Don't say that Carol!!
CAROL. Well, ever since Ellie passed, Chris has sort of taken a
dislike to me.
ARTHUR. She's just a teenager. It's the hormones.
CAROL. Maybe we rushed things Arthur—
ARTHUR. Now hold on a minute Carol—
CAROL. I'm just saying that maybe it wasn't right for us
To have started with our relations so fast after Ellie passed.

* See speciale note on songs and recordings on copyright page.

ARTHUR. It's been two months Carol!

CAROL. And with Chris going around hating me like that…
Oh Arthur, I don't think she's the only one who disapproves.
Your colleagues at the plant—

ARTHUR. They like you! Sure they like you, Carol.

CAROL. And those people from the country club—

ARTHUR. Well they're just a perfect example of rich people poor manners—

CAROL. Even the other nurses at work, I can just tell, they've cooled to me Arthur.
Perhaps they think I've taken advantage of a grief-stricken widower?

Arthur takes just a moment too long to respond.

ARTHUR. No, of course not.
I love you Carol.
And I suppose life has to go on…
Can't just sit here crying over spilled milk, can I?

A pause.

CAROL. I ought to go.

ARTHUR. What? No! Please don't Carol—

CAROL. They're all right, everybody's right about us—

ARTHUR. No, please stay Carol; I don't want to be alone!

CAROL. I'm taking advantage of you—

ARTHUR. You aren't!

CAROL. I just need to know whether I should stay or go Arthur.

ARTHUR. Stay.

A beat.

CAROL. Well then damn them all Arthur.
Damn all their nasty condescension.
What do they know about love, real love?

ARTHUR. Nothing. They don't know a thing.

CAROL. When love enters your life, you've got to be a real big fool to say no.

ARTHUR. That's true.

CAROL. We're just mortal. We're just all so mortal.
Who are we to say, "No love, go away from my heart right now, because my co-workers and my sullen teenage daughter disapprove."

ARTHUR. No one. No one at all.

CAROL. Oh Arthur, let's not wait then.

I don't need some silly old diamond ring, because I've got love.
ARTHUR. …
CAROL. Haven't I got love, Arthur?
ARTHUR. You do!
CAROL. I do! I can feel it.
We do! Wait, do you?
ARTHUR. I do?
CAROL. So do I!
Let's get married!
You're sure, I'm sure. What are we waiting for?

Arthur wants to protest but can't think of a good argument.

ARTHUR. Okay.
CAROL. Oh Arthur, do you really mean it?
ARTHUR. I do. I really do. You've got to be a real big fool to say no to love.
We'll just head on down to the chapel and that will be that.
CAROL. Oh, Arthur.
ARTHUR. I'm going to make an honest woman out of you Carol.
CAROL. Arthur, sweetheart.
ARTHUR. You and me and Chris will just head right down to the chapel and then we'll be a real family.

A pause.

CAROL. Do you really think we ought to bring Chris along?
She might not like it.
ARTHUR. Well, she's my daughter. And you're going to be her mother. Don't you think that's right?
CAROL. Well, I'm sure that whatever you think is right Arthur.
ARTHUR. You don't think it's right?
CAROL. You're the man in the family.
ARTHUR. Well—I just—what's your opinion about it?
CAROL. You're the boss Arthur. I won't impose myself. But I just think that Chris might not like it.

A pause.

ARTHUR. Maybe she wouldn't.
CAROL. Well don't let's not bring her on *my* account.
ARTHUR. No, you're probably right Carol. She might not feel comfortable.
She'll come around eventually though.

18

It's just those pesky hormones.
Isn't that right Carol?
CAROL. Oh Arthur, you've made me so happy!

> *She wraps her arms around him and kisses him. He picks her up and takes her upstairs. Shortly thereafter, we start to hear pretty loud sex sounds.*
>
> *Chris storms into the kitchen to escape the sex sounds. She sets her cassette player on the table and hits play. The song, like Pink Floyd's "Breathe,"* mostly muffles the sex sounds.*
>
> *She sits at the table, listening to the music. Finally the sex sounds reach a climax and stop.*
>
> *When she's sure it's really over, Chris notices her father's suit jacket, which he's left on one of the chairs. Chris puts it on, comforted.*
>
> *She disappears into the pantry and retrieves a candle.*
>
> *She lights the candle.*

CHRIS. Once upon a time, many many years ago in 1963,
A girl named Ellie lived in a little factory town in the Midwest
With her mom and dad, Nana and Gramps.

> *Very faintly, an animation starts to appear in the kitchen window, sketches that follow the story that Chris is telling. The drawings are flowing and vivid, slightly childlike but with a great deal of sorrow in them. Like a Chagall, or one of Lorca's sketches.*

More than anything, Ellie loved to sing and play the guitar.
But Nana and Gramps thought she ought to go to secretary school.
So one night, Ellie kissed her sleeping parents goodbye
And she got on a bus bound for San Francisco, California.
When she got there, she got a job in a bookstore during the day.
But every night she would go to a coffee place and sing and play the guitar onstage.
Then one night, a soldier named Arthur was on his way home from the war in Vietnam.
And on his way home, he stopped in San Francisco.
And one night while he was in San Francisco, he went to a coffee place.
And in that coffee place, he saw Ellie and heard her sing.

---

* See special note on songs and recordings on copyright page.

And he fell in love with her at first sight.

Animation Arthur falls in love with animation Ellie at first sight.

And so he decided not to go straight home to the Midwest, where Arthur also was from.

Instead, he stayed in San Francisco and tried to get Ellie to go out on a date with him.

And Ellie didn't really want to go on a date with him at first because Arthur could be a real square sometimes, but finally Ellie saw that Arthur had a warm smile

And was very persistent and so finally she said yes to a date,

And two weeks later they got married in San Francisco.

Then Ellie got pregnant,

And so they came back to the Midwest because their families wanted to be around Ellie's baby, which was me.

Chris closes her eyes and focuses hard.

Mom? Are you there?

This is your daughter, Christine.

If your spirit is present Ellie, please make that presence known somehow.

Ellie, this is your daughter Christine.

I love you and miss you so much.

If your spirit is present Ellie, please give me a sign.

Mom?

Disappointed, Chris puts her hands into her father's coat for warmth. Her fingers grasp something in the pocket. She pulls it out, and is amazed to find her mother's pearl necklace.

Ellie…

Chris smiles, blows out the candle, and runs back upstairs.

Blackout.

Scene 3

It's early the next morning. Carol comes downstairs in a crisp nurse's uniform. Today is the first day of the rest of her life! She starts to make some coffee. She calls upstairs.

CAROL. Chris?

> *No response.*

Chris are you up yet?
It's almost 7:30 and you wouldn't want to be tardy for school, would you?
Chris?

> *No response.*

I'm going to fix you some eggs and toast for breakfast, is that all right?

> *No response.*

Or would you rather just have some oatmeal and juice?
Chris?

> *Carol turns and sees that the pot from last night is back on the kitchen table, covered in dirt. She screams. Arthur calls down from upstairs.*

ARTHUR. Carol, honey you all right?
Hey Carol?

> *Carol seethes by the sink. Arthur lumbers down the stairs, a towel wrapped around his waist, half-shaven.*

What happened?

> *Carol does not respond. She just points to the pot on the table.*

Oh for the love of—Christine get down here!

> *No response. Arthur charges up the stairs. A moment later he drags Chris down the stairs in her pajamas.*

CHRIS. What?!?
ARTHUR. What do you mean, what?
Look at the table Christine; you see what I'm seeing?

CHRIS. Yeah.

ARTHUR. Why did you do that?

CHRIS. Do what?

ARTHUR. Why did you dig that back up and put it on the kitchen table?

CHRIS. I didn't do that.

ARTHUR. Then how do you explain the fact that it's sitting on the kitchen table?

CHRIS. I don't know. Maybe Carol did it.

CAROL. You're a liar.

You've been a very, very bad girl Christine. And what's more you're a liar because there is no other way that this pot could have gotten dug up and put back on this table other than you. You should be ashamed of yourself, you twisted little brat.

> *Carol is suddenly icy calm. She digs her nails into Chris's arm and pulls her in close.*

CHRIS. Arthur she's scratching me!

ARTHUR. Hey now Carol! Stop it!

CAROL. All I can say is thank goodness your poor mother isn't here to see what a horrible, nasty little girl you've become.

> *Chris bites Carol's arm, hard. Carol screams, throws Chris onto the floor.*

YOU BIT ME!! YOU EVIL LITTLE CUNT.

> *Chris screams and lunges back at Carol. Arthur gets between them.*

ARTHUR. Hey! Hey now.

Calm down.

Christine, apologize to Carol.

CHRIS. No way Dad. It was self defense.

ARTHUR. Carol, apologize to Christine.

CAROL. Are you insane?

Look at what she did Arthur.

> *I.e. the bite mark on her arm.*

You watched her kill that poor little animal last night.

She's merciless. You said yourself that you're scared of her.

And now she's done *this*, just to frighten me.

She's deranged. She's not normal, Arthur.

She's just being nasty and naughty and trying to get rid of me twelve ways to Sunday and you just keep taking her side.

ARTHUR. Did you dig up that pot Christine?

CHRIS. No.

ARTHUR. Then how'd it end up there?

A pause. Chris sees her opportunity and seizes it.

CHRIS. I dug it up.

CAROL. I knew it!

You see Arthur.

You're just a lying little troublemaker Christine.

CHRIS. I thought I'd clean up the pot for you Carol.

And give it to you as a wedding present.

Because I overheard you and Dad… talking… last night.

Congratulations, you guys.

Congratulations, Carol.

CAROL. …

CHRIS. You said at dinner how much you loved that pot, so I wanted to do something nice.

And I lied because I wanted it to be a surprise for you.

There's a big pause.

ARTHUR. Well.

CHRIS. I thought it would make you feel welcome, Carol.

ARTHUR. That was very thoughtful Christine.

CAROL. She's—

I know you're lying Christine.

You may be able to fool your father, but you can't fool me.

ARTHUR. Carol, that's enough.

Carol turns away from them, facing the sink. Chris starts to whimper.

CHRIS. She called me the C-word Dad. She scratched my arm up bad.

And all I wanted to do was help Carol out with her pot and give her a surprise.

Arthur goes over to comfort her.

ARTHUR. You just run along upstairs. There's some Bactine in the bathroom cabinet.

Finish getting ready and I'll drive you to school myself and maybe we'll even find time to pick up a Krispy Kreme on the way in.

Would you like that?

Chris nods and heads upstairs. As she leaves—

CHRIS. I'm really sorry you didn't like your present, Carol.

> *Chris goes. Carol is still facing the sink, with her back turned away from us.*

ARTHUR. Carol, it seems pretty clear to me that you overreacted.

CAROL. She drew blood you know.

And I'm going to have to get a suture probably.

It might even get infected.

Humans got dirtier mouths than dogs.

ARTHUR. You said some awful things to my child just now.

You owe her an apology.

> *Carol slowly turns back around to face Arthur. Suddenly she's back to Mrs. Brady on speedballs.*

CAROL. Oh Arthur, you're right.

I really botched that one up didn't I?

ARTHUR. What?

CAROL. It's—well, it's different times I suppose.

I don't have to tell you that back when you and I were growing up,

The sort of lip that she serves up would have gotten us a swift kick in our britches,

But times have changed right?

I suppose I'm just an old-fashioned kind of girl.

I just hope you and Chris will be able to find it in your hearts to forgive a poor old fuddy-duddy like me.

> *Carol tries to laugh it off again, like it's the end of the episode, but Arthur's not buying.*

ARTHUR. Carol, what's gotten into you?

CAROL. I feel just fine Arthur.

ARTHUR. This isn't funny.

CAROL. I'm so sorry Arthur. Honest to God I am.

> *A pause. She kisses him.*

Will you get rid of that awful thing Arthur? Will you do that for me?

> *Before she goes, she pauses and gives Arthur a kiss goodbye. Somehow the kiss escalates and the peck goodbye gets really hot and dirty. On both sides. Carol cuts it off—*

I'd best be going.

I just hope you have a good day at work Arthur.

Carol exits. Arthur takes the pot and shovel and heads out the back door.

Scene 4

It's later that afternoon, after school. Chris appears in the kitchen, in school clothes plus the pearl necklace. She gets an idea, goes out back, and retrieves Carol's pot. She hides it under the table, and admires her handiwork.

She notices a note on the refrigerator, grabs it, and starts to read it out loud.

CHRIS. Dear Christine. All I can say is how sorry I am for—blah blah blah fucking blah—
I hope you can find it in your heart to blah blah blah fuck you.
With love, Carol.
> *Chris takes a candle out of her backpack. She sits on the kitchen table and lights it, pops a tape into her cassette player, and hits play. It's a home recording...*

ELLIE. *Did you hit play?*
CHRIS. *Yeah.*
ELLIE. *You have to hit record and play.*
CHRIS. *Okay.*
ELLIE. *Are you ready?... I'm Ellie Cook.*
CHRIS. *And I'm Chris Cook.*
ELLIE. *And the name of our band is... do you want to say it?*
CHRIS. *The name of our band is—Captain Cook and Peter Pan!*
ELLIE. *And this is our latest hit single*
CHRIS. *(Title of song.)*
> *Chris and Ellie sing a bittersweet folk song such as "Mr. Tambourine Man."* Ellie accompanies them on the guitar. Chris is tentative at first, then becomes more confident. Ellie takes a verse or two on her own and she's wonderful. Her voice is*

---

* See special note on songs and recordings on copyright page.

beautiful and earthy and rich.

As the tape plays, Chris closes her eyes.

Once upon a time, last year in September
A woman named Ellie lived in this town, on this street, in this house
With her husband Arthur and her daughter Christine.

Another animation sequence plays out in the kitchen window. Animation Ellie, Arthur, and Chris share a happy family dinner.

When Ellie sang, you could feel the sound in your bones,
And when she laughed, she wrapped you up in a golden glow.

Then suddenly animation Ellie doubles over in pain.

But one night, Ellie got really sick.
So sick that Arthur had to drive her straight to the hospital.

We see animation Ellie in a hospital bed, surrounded by Arthur and Chris.

And when she got to the hospital,
The doctors took X-rays
And when they saw those X-rays,
The doctors shook their heads and called Arthur into their office to talk.

Arthur and Chris leave the room, sobbing.

Then Ellie got so sick that the doctors said
She better go home and rest.

We see Ellie in her bed, resting.

And then Carol came to take care of her,
And then—

Then a crude, nightmarish nurse figure with sharp teeth appears.

Then she—

The nurse raises a syringe like a dagger.

Then Carol—

The nurse stabs Ellie with the syringe repeatedly. Animation Ellie dies. Chris's eyes shoot open and she screams. She's panting, terrified.

Ellie? Did Carol…? Did she…?
I need a sign Ellie, please.

Chris waits. Nothing happens.

Please?

Hands shaking, Chris gives up and blows out the candle. Then Chris notices Carol's note on the counter.

Fucking Carol!

Furious, Chris strikes a match and lights it on fire. The blaze catches unexpectedly and there's more smoke. Chris throws it into the sink. The smoke detector starts to go off.

Shit.

She grabs the smoke detector and starts pulling the batteries out. The phone rings and rings and Chris doesn't answer it.

When the phone stops ringing, there's a moment of silence before we hear a rustling from the pot under the table. Chris hears it. Then it stops.

Maybe she's misheard? But there it is again, somewhere between the chirp of a baby bird and the whine of a newborn fox. As she approaches the pot, the sound gets louder.

She stands before the pot, braces herself and removes the lid. Several small animals start to scream in pain from the broad daylight.

Chris slams the lid back on, then opens it just a crack. The animals chatter happily.

Oh. My. God.
Mom?

There's a knock on the back door. Chris shoves the lid back down on the pot. From offstage—

HUGO. Hello?
CHRIS. Who's there?
HUGO. Hugo Schmidt.

Hugo Schmidt lets himself into the kitchen.

CHRIS. Jesus Hugo, you just walk into someone's house?
HUGO. My mother sent me.
She heard the… the ah, Feueralarm?
You are adequate? With the smoke?
CHRIS. Just peaches Hugo.
Had a little trash fire, nothing to write home about.

Hugo doesn't leave.

Goodbye Hugo.

> *The thing in the pot starts to make the chirping sound. It's loud enough so that they can both hear it. There's an awkward moment where they try to pretend that they didn't both hear it. But then—*

HUGO. Well. What is that?

CHRIS. Crickets. For my science fair project.

HUGO. And they are in the… pot?

CHRIS. You sure are nosy.

> *The sound again.*

HUGO. Okay. This is not crickets.

If you have small foxes or hens, you should free them from the pot lest they asphyxiate.

> *Chris removes the lid a little because she doesn't want them to die.*

Can I see?

CHRIS. I don't think so Hugo.

HUGO. I love all animals.

CHRIS. I just don't know if you're the sort of dork
That would tell on me to my dad if I showed you.

HUGO. I am not that sort of dork.

CHRIS. You sure?

HUGO. Ja.

CHRIS. Then you're gonna have to come close Hugo. I can only open it a crack.

They're not too keen on daylight. That's called nocturnal Hugo.

> *Chris removes the lid, and the creatures call out loudly. Chris and Hugo stare at the things in the pot, which are equally revolting and adorable. Then Chris gently places the lid half-way onto the pot.*

HUGO. *Oh. Mein. Gott.*

What is this?

CHRIS. Well Hugo, it's a pot full of beast-creatures with feathers and teeth.

HUGO. And big black eyes!

And eggshells?

CHRIS. They're hatching.
HUGO. They're revolting.
And adorable.
Where did you find them?
CHRIS. Well Hugo,
My father hit some weird thing with his car last night.
Then he put it in the pot then I stabbed it and they buried it.
But now it's back.
And it must have been carrying eggs when it died,
Because just now I'm noticing that there are many many more of them.
HUGO. This is what they are consuming?
CHRIS. This is what who are consuming?
HUGO. The meat they are consuming. It is their mother?

Chris had not considered this.

CHRIS. Yes. It seems like yes.
HUGO. There is almost no more left. What will you feed them?
CHRIS. Meat?

Chris goes to the refrigerator and takes out the silver bowl of ground beef. Hugo and Chris take turns making little wads of ground beef and tossing them into the cracked open pot. We can hear the animals eating.

HUGO. Wow. They have great hunger.
CHRIS. Yeah.

Hugo goes out on a limb, because he has a blazing crush on Chris and cannot believe she is actually talking to him.

HUGO. I… am sorry for your mother.
CHRIS. Me too Hugo.
HUGO. She was very beautiful and kind.
CHRIS. I know.
HUGO. What caused her death?
CHRIS. Carol. My dad's fiancée.

There's the jiggling of keys in the front door.

CAROL. Chris? Hon?

Chris slams the lid down on the pot, shoves it into Hugo's arms. Carol gets the door open—

CHRIS. Take this out back.

Hide it somewhere.

HUGO. Where?!

CHRIS. JUST HIDE IT SOMEWHERE Hugo.

And put a rock on the lid to make sure they can't escape.

HUGO. What about asphyxiation?

CHRIS. Leave it open a crack, but not so they can escape. GO!

Hugo vanishes just as Carol enters the kitchen carrying groceries.

As the following is happening upstairs, Hugo finds the entrance to the crawl space, jimmies it open and hides there with the pot.

CAROL. Who was that just now?

CHRIS. My friend.

CAROL. You have a friend?

CHRIS. Yes.

CAROL. What's your friend's name?

CHRIS. Pam.

CAROL. Why did Pam run away just now?

CHRIS. She had to get home in time for supper.

CAROL. How was school?

CHRIS. Fine. How was your job?

CAROL. Good. Did you get the note I left you?

I'd like it if we could be friends…

Chris heads upstairs.

Why does it smell like smoke in here?

Carol notices the box of matches on the kitchen table.

Wait, were you smoking cigarettes?

Were you and your friend Pam sneaking cigarettes?

And that's how come she shot out of here like that?

Carol is sort of impressed.

Cigarettes. Well. You could have just said so.

I didn't know you were into that sort of thing.

As Chris leaves—

Your dad won't be home for half an hour…

You want to have a cigarette with me?

Chris doesn't leave. Carol goes into her purse and takes out a pack of cigarettes. She offers one to Chris. After a beat, Chris takes it. Carol lights it for her. Chris has clearly never smoked before.

You have to inhale.

> *Chris inhales and starts coughing violently.*

Not in your lungs so much.

> *Chris gets it under control. Carol lights one for herself and takes a big drag. Surprised, delighted.*

Never thought I'd see this day.
So what do you think?
CHRIS. About smoking?
CAROL. Sure.
CHRIS. It's cool.

> *Hugo calls out into the darkness of the crawl space. Chris and Carol can both hear him.*

HUGO. Hello?
CAROL. What was that?
CHRIS. What was what?
CAROL. Is there someone in the crawl space?

> *Chris ignores this.*

I know things have been pretty strained between us and I just hope that maybe this can be a new beginning.

> *Chris notices Carol's arm is bandaged where she bit her earlier.*

They bandaged my arm up today at work.
I'm on oral antibiotics for a couple of days just to be sure, but I should really be just fine.

> *They smoke in silence for a moment. Chris stares suspiciously at Carol.*

I don't know whether or not you read my note Christine, but I really am sorry.
It was wrong of me to call you a liar. And those other things that I said… they were terrible. Please forgive me?
CHRIS. Sure Carol.
CAROL. Wow. We're talking.
I just can't believe we're actually talking.
It's really nice.
CHRIS. Sure Carol.
CAROL. You know,
If you ever feel that you'd like to talk about your mother, about Ellie, I'm here for you. That's not just lip service.

31

I can imagine it's a real puzzling and a real hard time for you?

No response.

You meet so many different people doing what I do Chris,
But your mother was special.
She and I got real close those last few days.
It's an intimate type thing, going into someone's home to watch over their passing.
Doing everything in my power to make them feel... comfortable.
CHRIS. Comfortable?
CAROL. Mmm-hmm.
CHRIS. Comfortable how Carol?
CAROL. Those treatments, well, you know as well as I do, those treatments are almost worse than the cancer itself.
Sometimes when people are very sick,
Sick like Ellie was,
My job is to give them medicine that makes them more...
Comfortable.

This information crashes down on Chris.

But your mother fought hard and she didn't want to give up because she had you.
CHRIS. So then why did she die?
CAROL. Well.
CHRIS. If she was so strong and she was such a fighter how come she died?
CAROL. This is very hard, I know.
CHRIS. I know that you know, Carol.
CAROL. What's that Chris?

Chris stands, silently trying to contain her grief and rage. She paces around the kitchen. Finally she stands staring Carol straight in the eyes. She does not break eye contact as she extinguishes her cigarette on her own forearm. She doesn't scream.

When it's over, she tosses the cigarette on the ground.

CHRIS. Go to hell Carol.
You're a filthy fucking liar and I see right through you.
CAROL. Well.
If that's how you feel about it, then all right.

Chris starts to head upstairs.

Note: However this is staged, the audience should not be able to see Carol's eyes directly.

Carol calls after Chris—

Chris, hon?

Chris turns around and looks over her shoulder to meet Carol's gaze. A horrible, animal moment passes between them.

CHRIS. What just happened with your eyes Carol?

CAROL. My eyes?

CHRIS. Your eyes went black Carol.

CAROL. What are you saying Chris?

CHRIS. Like two black holes Carol, I've never seen anything so horrible in my life.

A beat.

CAROL. Sounds like somebody needs a nap Chris.
Why don't you go have a lie-down Chris? Rest up before supper.

Chris backs out of the kitchen and runs up the stairs. Carol very calmly starts to unpack the groceries she's bought. It's all manner of meat products: bacon, chicken legs, hot dogs, cold cuts, and a whole lot of ground beef.

Scene 5

A little later. Dinnertime. Carol and Chris, with matching bandages on their arms, flank Arthur at the table.

ARTHUR. Christine,
Carol told me about your accident.
She said you burned your arm helping her make supper?
Well it was very nice of you to offer to help.
I'm glad you two were able to make up and be friends.
There's something that I—that we—need to tell you Christine.
It's actually a bit of good news.
Carol and I got to talking just now and well, you've got to be a real big fool to say no to love. Right, Carol?

CAROL. A real big fool.

ARTHUR. We've decided, and I think you'll actually be happy about this, we've decided that we just don't want to wait and throw a whole big wedding.

So we're skipping the chapel!

Carol and I are heading right down to city hall tomorrow morning and we're going to get married and come back and be a real family.

Because a young girl needs a mother, Chris.

I know you do.

What do you think about that?

CHRIS. Dad, I'm going to say something right now, and I know you're not going to like it.

But just remember when I say it that you've known me for thirteen years and you've known Carol for three days and two months.

Carol killed Mom. And also I think she might not be human. Please don't marry her.

ARTHUR. Christine—

CHRIS. You know how I know this? Here's why:

Mom was sick, but she was getting better.

Then Carol decided she wanted to take Mom's place.

So Carol made Mom really sick for those last three days.

And made her so weak that she couldn't fight back those last three days.

And now Mom is dead and Carol's marrying you.

CAROL. That's fine. / That's just fine Arthur.

ARTHUR. You're still young Christine,

But you're old enough that you should know the weight and the implication of slandering another person in that way.

Put yourself in Carol's shoes.

Here she is, trying the best she knows how to take care of us, to be a family with us and you sit there and accuse her of murdering your mother.

How would you feel if you were Carol?

CHRIS. I would feel scared. Because the truth was finally coming out.

CAROL. Arthur, I'm going. I'm going to pack my things and I'm going to go.

ARTHUR. Hold on a second Carol, we're going to figure this out.

CAROL. No, we're not.

CHRIS. If it's not true, then say it's not true Carol.

CAROL. I won't dignify that with a response.

CHRIS. She won't say it's not true because she knows she did it.

ARTHUR. That's not why she won't say it.

CHRIS. Remember when we used to be a family with just you me and Mom?

You can't get that back by marrying your wife's killer.

ARTHUR. That'll do Christine.

Arthur tries to ignore her. Chris starts to lose it.

CHRIS. You have to believe me Dad, I'm your daughter!

You used to love Mom so much.

Do you love Carol just the same as you loved Ellie?

She murdered Mom.

HAVE YOU LOST YOUR MIND DAD?

ARTHUR. Shut up!

Arthur suddenly shoves Chris, knocking her to the floor.

CHRIS. SHE'S SOME SORT OF FUCKING ANIMAL DAD! SHE CAN MAKE HER EYES TURN INTO BLACK HOLES IF SHE FEELS LIKE IT. HER EYES GO BLACK. I SAW HER DO IT JUST THIS AFTERNOON.

CAROL. Oh God / Arthur—

ARTHUR. Go to your room Christine.

Chris is up in a flash, at the knife drawer. She pulls out the big knife from last night and goes after Carol. Arthur grabs Chris just as she's about to lunge at Carol, who, at the last possible moment, holds out her hands to protect herself—

CAROL. I'm pregnant!

Arthur don't let her hurt me, I'm pregnant.

ARTHUR. What?

CAROL. This morning Arthur, remember how I was acting funny?

Well I got worried and thought something might not be right.

It turned out it was the hormones.

I took the test today, and I'm pregnant.

Oh God.

I won't put our child in harm's way Arthur.

Carol grabs her bag and heads for the door.

ARTHUR. Carol, stop.

CAROL. It's not safe for me here Arthur.

Look what she's capable of.

Oh I am so afraid!

Carol starts sobbing.

ARTHUR. Go wait in the car Carol, I'll take care of this.

CAROL. It's her or me. One of us has got to go Arthur—

ARTHUR. Carol, go wait in the car.

> *Carol exits. Arthur is left holding Chris, who is still holding the knife.*

Put down the knife Christine.

> *Chris puts it down.*

CHRIS. Dad—

ARTHUR. I want you to listen to me very carefully Christine.
You're at a crossroads here.
You choose to keep going down the road you're on,
Then I can't make any promises about what's going to happen to you.
I know you loved Ellie. I loved Ellie too.
But you just tried to stab the woman who is carrying my child.
Carol and I are going to go for a drive now.
We'll be back in a couple of hours.
While we're gone, you're going to pack your things.
And when we get back,
I'm going to either drive you to Grandma and Pops' house, or to a hospital.
Your call.

CHRIS. How long do I have to go away for?

ARTHUR. …

CHRIS. Dad, please don't do this to me.

ARTHUR. …

> *Arthur exits. Chris sinks onto the floor, numb.*
>
> *Then there's a knock on the kitchen floor.*

HUGO. Ah… This is Hugo Schmidt speaking.

CHRIS. Jesus.

HUGO. I have concealed myself with the pot beneath your home.

CHRIS. Just leave the pot down there and go home Hugo.

HUGO. Ah, yes well.
It seems their appetite has increased.
Perhaps you might bring them more of the meat?

> *Chris goes to the fridge and pulls out ground beef, chicken legs, hot dogs, bacon, and cold cuts. She grabs a couple of flashlights*

out of the pantry.

She goes out the back door and reappears in the crawl space.

CHRIS. You picked a good hiding place Hugo.

HUGO. It is the Luftschutzkeller, no?
This is something in most homes?
In case of bomb attacks?

CHRIS. It's the crawl space.
There aren't bomb attacks in America.

The things in the pot start chirping and whining loudly.

HUGO. Perhaps they can smell the food.

Illuminated only by flashlights, Hugo and Chris remove the pot's lid and shine the flashlights into the pot. Chris tries to feed the animals. The animals scream.

CHRIS. Come on, little beasties.

They do not eat.

HUGO. Huh.

CHRIS. Put down your flashlight, Hugo.

He does. They eat.

Whoa. Now they're really hungry. See, Hugo? Nocturnal.

HUGO. They are robust.

CHRIS. Wow. Are they…? Have they gotten bigger since?

HUGO. I thought perhaps this was typical for this species—

CHRIS. Yeah, probably. Right?

HUGO. Yeah. Probably.
From my perspective, it seems that when we feed the species, their hunger increases.

CHRIS. Yeah. From my perspective too Hugo.

Chris dangles a chicken leg above the pot. Something black and half-seen pops up from the pot and grabs it, slicing open her hand as it does so. Her hand starts to bleed. The animals' cries become frenzied.

Little shit ball!
That little beast just tore my hand open!

She slams the lid down onto the pot and the sound of the animals is muffled. Hugo grabs her hand—

HUGO. Here let me.

37

And starts sucking on the wound—Boy-Scout snake-bite-style—to stop the bleeding.

You must put some ah—peroxide on it, so that it does not become inflamed.

CHRIS. Something terrible's happened Hugo.

HUGO. I dropped the eaves from here of what you said to your Papa.

CHRIS. Carol isn't just a murderer Hugo.

HUGO. No.

CHRIS. I saw something today that I can never unsee.

HUGO. Her eyes?

Chris nods.

Perhaps Carol is Teufel?

CHRIS. What the hell's a Teufel Hugo?

HUGO. A devil.

When I was small child, my Großmutter told me stories about Teufel.

CHRIS. I don't think we have Teufels in America.

HUGO. During the war in my country, she said

There were Teufel that disguised themselves in human form.

They snatched people from their homes in the night and burned them. Their hearts were ice, and their eyes were black pitch pots. And no one believed they were real until much too late. The Teufels stole her husband, and two of her sons.

CHRIS. That's Nazis, not devils.

Right?

Hugo shrugs.

What did your grandma say to do about Teufels?

HUGO. This part was past my bedtime.

CHRIS. Do you think I'm crazy Hugo?

HUGO. No.

CHRIS. That's good.

HUGO. So what will you do?

CHRIS. I have to kill Carol.

HUGO. You jest?

CHRIS. No jest Hugo. You're a Boy Scout right? Eye for an eye. It's justice.

HUGO. It is terrible.

CHRIS. You know what's terrible Hugo?

Watching your mom die slowly because your future stepmom poisoned her.

And then having to go live somewhere else because your Teufel stepmom is brainwashing your dad.

HUGO. How will you deliver the justice?

CHRIS. I don't know yet Hugo.

HUGO. And how will you be rid of Carol's body?

There's a hungry little animal grumble from inside the pot.

CHRIS. The more they eat, the hungrier they get.
Right Hugo?

HUGO. Right.

CHRIS. They're getting bigger by the minute.
Pretty soon they're going to be hungrier for more than just hot dogs.

HUGO. Much hungrier.

CHRIS. I bet these little monsters could eat their way
Through one hundred ten pounds of pure bullshit in no time flat.

A beat.

I think my mom sent me a bunch of little beast creatures in a pot
So that they could eat Carol, Hugo.

HUGO. Wait. What?!!

CHRIS. There'd be no trace left of her, and nobody would ever have to find out.
It's probably the only way to even kill a Teufel Hugo.

HUGO. Ah…

CHRIS. Godzilla v. Mothra
Dr. Frankenstein v. Monster
Beast creatures v. Carol
Ellie, they're perfect!
This could be our little secret. Would you like that Hugo?

HUGO. I don't know.

CHRIS. Don't be a little shit Hugo.

HUGO. I am not a small shit.

CHRIS. I'm not so sure about that Hugo.

HUGO. Why?

CHRIS. I see you at school Hugo, I see you on the bus.

HUGO. I have also seen you on the bus. And many times I have watched you at school.

CHRIS. You're not a cool guy Hugo.

HUGO. I am very cool.

CHRIS. What kind of music do you listen to Hugo?

HUGO. Ah, Beethoven? Polka? Petunia Clark?

39

CHRIS. Who the hell is Petunia Clark?

Hugo sings in a very high-pitched voice.

HUGO. When you're alone and life is making you lonely you could always go
Down-town.
CHRIS. You are not cool Hugo.
HUGO. No.
CHRIS. I bet you'd like to be cool Hugo.

Hugo would really like to be cool.

I think there's a simple solution here.
I'll be your friend, you help me kill Carol.
HUGO. But—
CHRIS. All you have to do is help feed the animals Hugo.
You wouldn't even be doing anything bad.
HUGO. I cannot do this Christine…

Chris musses Hugo's hair till it looks cooler. Hugo can't believe she's touching him.

CHRIS. I just made you five times cooler Hugo. You owe me.
HUGO. It is not bad to feed animals.
CHRIS. It's a kindness Hugo.
HUGO. Okay.
CHRIS. Okay!
HUGO. What do we do?

The animals in the pot whine with hunger.

CHRIS. We go find them some food.
HUGO. What food?
CHRIS. They eat meat.
HUGO. We're out of meat.
CHRIS. You know that lady up the street with all those cats?
HUGO. Yes.
CHRIS. Well, we're going to need some trash bags Hugo.

Hugo and Chris exit the crawl space.

Scene 6

Just a little while later, Hugo and Chris stumble into the kitchen. They've both got some blood and some cat fur stuck to them. Hugo carries a couple of cat collars.

HUGO. Oh God Christine, I will be sick—
CHRIS. You did a good job Hugo.
HUGO. Oh Christine, the meowing! And the crunching. The poor little kitty pussies!
CHRIS. We're not looking back Hugo.
HUGO. I think the pot will not contain them any longer.
CHRIS. They're getting stronger Hugo, that's a good thing.

> *There's a loud banging and howling sound from the crawl space. Then the sound of a car pulling up to the curb outside. Arthur and Carol get out.*

ARTHUR. Chris? Chris hon, are you there?
HUGO. Oh Gott. What do we do?
CHRIS. I'll think of something Hugo.
ARTHUR. Chris? Hon?
CHRIS. It's all going to work out Hugo.

> *Arthur starts to unlock the door. Hugo panics and hides in the pantry. Chris runs upstairs just as Arthur and Carol enter the kitchen.*

ARTHUR. Christine?
We're back now.
You all packed up?

> *No response.*

Christine?

> *Nothing.*

She must still be upstairs.
I'll go check on her Carol, won't take me but a moment.
CAROL. Please don't leave me Arthur, I'm afraid.

ARTHUR. We're going to get all of this sorted out Carol.
CHRISTINE!
CAROL. I'm sure she'll be down in a minute.

> *Carol fiddles anxiously around the kitchen, cleaning things. Arthur reaches into his pocket.*

ARTHUR. There's something I've been meaning to give you Carol.

> *Arthur takes a small box out of his pocket.*

CAROL. Oh Arthur what's this now?
ARTHUR. I think it might be a source of comfort to you,
And a promise that I'm a man of my word.
Go ahead and open it.

> *Carol opens the box. Her reaction quickly turns from delight to a sort of horror.*

CAROL. Oh, Arthur.
ARTHUR. Don't you like it?
CAROL. It's lovely Arthur.
Only, isn't this the same necklace that Ellie used to wear?
ARTHUR. That one belongs to Chris now.
I took hers to the jeweler and had him make a replica for you.
It's just like the one I gave to Ellie the day we were married.
Shall I help you put it on?
CAROL. Well it's such a sweet gesture but I'm not sure that's right
Arthur…

> *There's a loud thumping and scratching sound from the crawl space.*

Did you hear that?
ARTHUR. It's an old house Carol. Could be the water heater.
CAROL. Oh. Well then.
ARTHUR. You're probably right about the necklace Carol. It was so foolish of me to do that.
CAROL. No, no hon it was such a sweet gesture. It's only—
Well if it'll make you happy Arthur I'll wear it.
ARTHUR. No, it was just so foolish Carol.
CAROL. Will you help me with the clasp?

> *Arthur takes the necklace out of the box and puts it on Carol.*

ARTHUR. You look beautiful.

> *Carol goes in to embrace Arthur. He demurs.*

CAROL. Arthur sweetheart what's the matter?

ARTHUR. Oh Carol, I know I shouldn't do it,

But sometimes I still think about what happened with Ellie.

CAROL. You know it's no use looking back Arthur.

ARTHUR. She struggled so at the end Carol—

CAROL. She was suffering so—

ARTHUR. So frail that something as soft as a pillow—

CAROL. What you did was a kindness Arthur.

ARTHUR. You sure Carol?

CAROL. I'm sure.

> *He hugs Carol.*

ARTHUR. Carol, I know you and Chris have had some… run-ins lately.

I mean hell, we've had some pretty serious run-ins in this house lately—

CAROL. That's putting it pretty mildly Arthur.

ARTHUR. But honest to God Carol, I believe that Chris really is a good girl.

She's just been having a hard time lately, with the hormones and all—

CAROL. I don't want to talk about Chris anymore.

ARTHUR. If you'd have met Chris before Ellie got sick.

She was… night and day.

She was just the most curious, beautiful child you'd ever seen

She had these joyful green eyes…

CAROL. Arthur.

ARTHUR. Then with everything that happened, well…

She's obviously very different now.

I know it's going to take some time for all of this to heal,

But I really do believe that you, me, and Chris will be a family one day.

CAROL. And the baby?

ARTHUR. You betcha.

When I met you Carol I just thought to myself,

Here is a woman who is so kind and so good

Maybe she could help as a sort of mother to Chris bring some light back into those green eyes?

> *A pause.*

CAROL. Is that what you thought when you met me Arthur?

ARTHUR. You're just so gentle and good Carol.
CAROL. I thought you loved me Arthur.
ARTHUR. Well yeah, that too.

> *A pause.*

CAROL. Can't just bring Chris's eyes back from the dead, can I? No crying over spilt milk?

> *In the crawl space, the pot seems like it's about to burst. The crawl space is almost roaring now.*

ARTHUR. Did you hear that Carol?
CAROL. You said yourself it's just the water heater Arthur.
ARTHUR. Might be a possum got stuck in the crawl space.
CAROL. Doesn't sound like any possum I've ever heard Arthur.
ARTHUR. No, I reckon not Carol. Best go check on it. Won't be a minute.

> *Arthur exits to go investigate the crawl space. Carol lights a cigarette and sits at the table. Arthur reappears at the entrance to the crawl space. Using only a lighter to guide his way, Arthur approaches the howling pot.*

Oh my—what is that *smell?*
Carol! Hey Carol hon.
You know of any reason why your pot is in the crawl space?
CAROL. No.
ARTHUR. Carol hon, you best call animal control. There's something living in the pot.
CAROL. In the pot Arthur?
Didn't you bury it?

> *The animals can smell Arthur and are going wild. They're just about to burst through the pot—*

ARTHUR. It's ah, I'm coming up now Carol.
Oh heck, of all the times for my lighter to go out.
Carol?!

> *Arthur's lighter goes out. In the dark, the pot tips over and the animals escape. We hear what sounds like dozens of squealing animals released from the pot. In the darkness we hear the sound of screaming and grisly eating sounds. Then no screams and just eating—*

CAROL. Arthur? Are you alright?

After the eating ends, we suddenly start to hear the sound of many small animals all around. They've crawled into the walls, the floor, the ceiling, into all the bones of the house. It's impossible to ignore.

Chris runs downstairs, terrified.

CHRIS. Dad?!

Carol turns to her—

CAROL. Hello Christine.

Then suddenly Hugo bursts out of the cabinet, brandishing two cans of Raid as weapons. He streams Raid into Carol's face as Carol screams. Carol passes out, hits her head on the floor, and starts bleeding.

HUGO. Oh no. Oh no. Oh no. Oh no.

He goes to staunch Carol's wound, gets blood all over his hands. It's sticky.

It's sticky…

Chris bangs on the floor above the crawl space.

CHRIS. Arthur?!? Are you there?

She presses her ear to the floor, there's no response. She collapses into sobs for a moment.

Then there's a rustling sound from the walls. Hugo shrieks.

HUGO. What is that scratching sound in the walls?
CHRIS. The animals must have gotten into the walls Hugo.
HUGO. Oh Gott! She needs a doctor.
CHRIS. We're going to have to restrain her Hugo.
Until I can figure out what to do.
HUGO. Eins, zwei, drei.

They lift Carol onto a chair. Chris duct tapes Carol to the chair.

What about your Papa Chris?
Did not you hear him in the Luftschutzkeller?

Chris nods.

We must help him Chris.
CHRIS. Didn't sound like there was anything left to help.

HUGO. Your mama was beautiful and kind.
Why would your mama's beast creatures wreak such horror upon
your Papa Chris?
CHRIS. What if these aren't my mother's beast creatures Hugo?
HUGO. But if they are not your mother's beast creatures Chris,
What are they?

>*Carol momentarily regains consciousness.*

CAROL. She's mad.
Oh little boy, she's crazy, please don't let her kill me.
HUGO. You killed her mama.
CAROL. Her mother died of Breast Cancer.
Please!
CHRIS. SHUT UP CAROL!!
HUGO. I will phone the police.
CAROL. That's right honey, call the police. Do it right now. I need
to see a doctor right away—

>*Carol slips out of consciousness.*

CHRIS. No police Hugo.
HUGO. What? Why?!
CHRIS. Because I know just what they'll say.
It happens all the time on TV.
There's no proof.
They'll let her go and she'll move on to another town and do this to
someone else.
HUGO. She will be tried.
The police will deliver justice.

>*Hugo goes for the phone, Chris yanks it out of his hand and
>smashes it on the kitchen floor.*

CHRIS. I'm all alone now and she's the reason why.
You want to set her free?
HUGO. You are not all alone.

>*Hugo grabs Chris's face and kisses her. Chris is stunned.*

You must stop this now Christine.
I am sorry but I cannot continue to be complicit in this tragedy.

>*Hugo goes for the door. In a panic, Chris tackles him and pins
>him to the floor. She manages to get him in a headlock, and*

drags him kicking and screaming into the pantry. She props a chair against the door so he can't open it.

CHRIS. JUST SHUT UP FOR JUST ONE SECOND HUGO! You don't have to be a part of this but I can't let her go. I'm going to figure all this out Hugo.

HUGO. It is so dark in this pantry Christine.

Then we start to hear the scratching sound again.

I think that the animals are—Christine, you must free me from the pantry.

It is so dark Christine!

Soon we just hear Hugo's screams and the sound of eating. Chris tries frantically to get the door open but it's stuck. Then no more screams and just eating. Then they retreat back into the walls. After a moment, Chris opens the pantry door. A pool of blood oozes out onto the kitchen floor.

Chris picks up what's left of Hugo's bones. She goes offstage for a moment, returns with the shovel, then exits out the back door with the bones and the shovel.

Scene 7

A little while later. Carol sits passed out, still duct taped to the chair. The opening strains of a song like Pink Floyd's "Wish You Were Here" start to play from upstairs.* Carol rouses. She notices the blood on the floor. She screams.

She struggles in her chair, tries to tear at the tape with her teeth. She squirms her way over to the knife drawer, pulls it open. She manages to get one out, but then drops it. We suddenly notice that Chris has been silently watching this. She's carrying her cassette player and wearing one of Carol's nursing uniforms and a gas mask. Chris very calmly walks over to the oven and turns on the gas.

CAROL. CHRIS!?!
Oh Chris, for the love of God!

> *Suddenly, Chris starts to dance along with the song. It's an incredibly weird dance, sort of like a ritual shamanic grief trance. She just dances to the song over Carol and seems not to notice a word she's saying.*

Chris honey, listen to me.
What happened to that little boy who was here before?
Is that his blood on the floor?
What happened here Chris?
You did something to him.
Oh no, I think that you did…
Okay, it doesn't matter, it's all going to be okay.
You're in way over your head, I can see that.
But I can help you if you'll let me.
You've had a very bad trauma Chris.
This is not my opinion, it's medical fact.
And trauma can make people act in ways that are unhinged.
But nobody is blaming you. It's perfectly understandable.
You need to let me go so that I can get you some help, and so that

---

* See special note on songs and recordings on copyright page.

I can get some help for Arthur if he needs it.
Your mother loved you very much Chris.
Even in the midst of this tragedy, you're lucky.
Because you've been loved.
That's something that not everyone gets.
Don't dishonor her memory by... hurting me.
I never even knew my parents—

       Chris abruptly stops.

CHRIS. Then where'd you get the pot?

CAROL. What?

CHRIS. Where'd you get your mother's pot from?

CAROL. I was adopted.

CHRIS. Liar.

CAROL. Chris, could we please not mince words at the moment
because
RIGHT NOW I AM OUT OF MY HEAD!
I've ingested a whole lot of Raid, which could kill me.
The oven is slowly filling this room with gas, which could also kill me.
My head is bleeding.
For all I know, Arthur is dead.
I am currently pregnant,
And you duct taped me to a chair and possibly killed a little boy too.
Please?
Please?
Let me help you with all of this.
You're not alone.

CHRIS. I am Carol. And it's your fault. And that's why you have
to die.

CAROL. You think Ellie would have wanted this?
Do you know something that your mother told me?
She told me about the New Year's Eve when you had that terrible
fever, and you were delirious, and you kept asking her to sing
"Octopus's Garden" over and over again and how it got stuck in
Arthur's head for months.

CHRIS. Stop talking Carol.

CAROL. She told me that the two of you used to go on adventures
together.
She said that when you were eleven she took you to a Grateful
Dead concert in Cincinnati, even though your dad said you were
too little.

I could take you to go see the Grateful Dead.

CHRIS. She told you that?

CAROL. She sure did Chris.

She said she named you Christine after her best friend in elementary school.

That you used to stay up all night watching old episodes of *The Twilight Zone* and how one time you got so scared you thought Arthur was a zombie.

How your favorite color is blue, and how she wished she could have seen the Grand Canyon.

I'll be Captain Cook if you'll be Peter Pan...

>   *Chris stares at Carol, frozen. A beat.*

>   *Chris panics, goes into the pantry for a candle, tries to light it.*

WHAT ARE YOU DOING CHRISTINE?!? THE GAS.

>   *Chris puts down the candle and the match. She notices the necklace Carol is wearing.*

CHRIS. That's my mom's necklace.

CAROL. What?

CHRIS. The necklace you're wearing.

It was Ellie's.

In this whole wide world, there was only one necklace like that, because it was special.

Because she loved it.

Why do you have this?

CAROL. Maybe she wanted me to have it, Chris.

>   *This stops Chris.*

CHRIS. Did you kill her?

CAROL. No honey, I didn't.

>   *A beat as this sinks in.*

CHRIS. Oh no. Oh no. Oh no. Oh no. Oh no.

If I let you go, will I get electrocuted for letting the animals eat Arthur and Hugo?

They'll electrocute me, won't they?

CAROL. Hey there hon... hey, it's going to be okay.

Where are their bodies?

CHRIS. Hugo's bones are buried out back next to the grill.

The animals got all the rest.

CAROL. That's… you know what that's good Chris.
There's a silver lining here.
That's evidence for the police that the animals did it.
CHRIS. Really?
CAROL. Yeah. They taught me all about this kind of stuff in nursing school.
The police can just take a swab and they'll know right away that it was an animal because of the bacteria. They'll know right away that it wasn't you.
Okay?
Everything's going to be okay.
CHRIS. They can tell from a swab?
CAROL. They sure can.

> *Chris turns off the gas. A shadow woman appears in the window. Chris doesn't see her.*

Good girl.
CHRIS. My mom had such a beautiful voice.
This one time when I was seven, I asked her why I didn't have any brothers or sisters and she told me it was because she knew she couldn't love anybody else as much as she loved me.
She used to make fun of my dad for liking country music, but this one time I found them slow-dancing in the backyard to a Johnny Cash song.
She smelled like… my mom.
And I'll never smell her smell again as long as I live.
CAROL. Oh hun.

> *The shadow woman starts to bang and claw at the window in total silence.*

Chris hon, help me help you.
Untape me from the chair sweetheart.
CHRIS. You'll hurt me.
CAROL. No honey I won't.
CHRIS. I'm going to be in so much trouble.
CAROL. I will protect you, I promise.
Come here.

> *Chris shakes her head no.*

You're not alone pumpkin.
You've got me and I've got you.

Chris slowly makes her way over to Carol.

You see? Everything is okay.

I'm not mad.

In the morning, this will all be like a bad dream.

> *Chris nods. She kneels in front of Carol and places her head on Carol's lap.*

Good girl Chris. Everything is going to be okay.

> *Then very suddenly, Carol crosses one leg over the other and starts choking Chris with her thighs. Chris fights, but Carol squeezes harder, and then after a moment it's over.*

> *The shadow woman watches this happen, powerless and horrified.*

> *Chris rolls to the floor. Carol tips over in her chair, retrieves the knife from the floor, and cuts herself loose. The shadow woman disappears.*

> *Carol takes a moment to survey the wreckage in the kitchen. She rubs her belly, and all of a sudden we can hear the strange chirping of the newborn animals in the pot.*

> *Then Carol very deliberately turns off the lights in the kitchen. She exits.*

> *In the dark, we hear the sounds of scraping and scrabbling all around.*

End of Play

PROPERTY LIST

National Geographic magazine
Cigarettes and lighter
Burnt pot roast
Pot with lid
Potholders, metal bowl, and tea towel
Box of Hamburger Helper and package of ground beef
Rubber gloves, Ajax, and a scrubbing brush
Large carving knife
Chinese takeout containers and chopsticks
Flashlights
Candle and matches
Pearl necklace and small box
Shovel
Note
Cassette player
Smoke detector
Meat products, including bacon, chicken legs, hot dogs, cold cuts, and ground beef.
Backpack
Purse
Cat collars
Duct tape
2 cans of Raid
Bones
Gas mask

SOUND EFFECTS

Front door opening
Loud music from record player
Smoke detector alarm
Phone ringing
Car pulling up
Creature sounds: whining, scratching, snarling, screaming, rustling,
    chirping, eating, banging, howling, and thumping

9780822235538